This Weather Is No Womb

ALSO BY PARKER TOWLE

Search for Doubloons: Wings Press, 1981 (chapbook)

Handwork: Nightshade Press, 1991 (chapbook)

Our Places: Andrew Mountain Press, 1998 (chapbook)

Exquisite Reaction (anthology): Andrew Mountain Press, 2000 (edited)

The Worcester Review, special section on Frank O'Hara, 2001 (edited)

The Worcester Review, special section on Stanley Kunitz, 2005 (co-edited)

THIS WEATHER IS NO WOMB

Poems

by

Parker Towle

Antrim House
Simsbury, Connecticut

Copyright © 2007
by Parker Towle

Except for short selections reprinted for purposes of
book review, all reproduction rights are reserved.
Requests for permission to replicate should
be addressed to the publisher.

Library of Congress Cataloging-in-Publication Data

Towle, Parker, 1933-
This weather is no womb : poems / by Parker Towle. -- 1st ed.
p. cm.
ISBN 978-0-9792226-2-7 (alk. paper)
I. Title.

PS3570.O897T48 2007
811'.54--dc22
                      2007025821

Printed & bound by Sheridan Books, Inc.

First edition, 2007

Cover painting by Paula Wolcott
Photographs by Berton Towle (p. 13), Paula Wolcott (p. 31),
Parker Towle (pp. 51, 83) and Phyllis Towle (cover)

Antrim House
860.217.0023
AntrimHouse@comcast.net
www.AntrimHouseBooks.com
P.O. Box 111, Tariffville, CT 06081

Dedicated to my mother

Pearl A. Towle

fully able, gratefully, at age 100
to tell me exactly what she likes
and does not like about this collection

ACKNOWLEDGEMENTS

The poems in this collection first appeared in the following publications, sometimes in earlier versions:

Beacon Review: "Love Poem"
Body Language (anthology): "Cases"
Buckle &: "Requiem for a Marine and His Mate"
Calliope: "Variations on a Riff by Eubie Blake, Dead Age 100, 1984"
Calypso: "At the Hiroshima Hospital"
Cape Rock: "To the Boy with the Flying Hair"
Common Ground Review: "Green Mountain Solo," "Honduran Mission"
The Contemporary Review: "Mango and the Moon"
Dartmouth Medicine: "Generation"
Ecossaise (anthology): "One Night Late Fall"
Entelechy International: "Footprints"
The Galley Sail Review: "Hooking Rugs and Ice-Fishing," "The Incredible"
Green Hills Literary Lantern: "Centenarian" (as "Mercy")
Green Mountain Trading Post: "Buck," "The Drive to Putnamville"
Hodge Podge Poetry: "Dusk, a Stream, and a White Owl Cigar"
Handwork (chapbook): "Speck Pond's Light," "Madison Gulf"
Images from Ruin (anthology): "The Architecture of Nine-Eleven"
It's All the Rage (anthology): "To a Friend Who Loves Trucks"
The Kerf: "A Drowning"
Lifelines: "Evening," "Cases" (as "The Profession")
The Lucid Stone: "Fantasy," "What's It Like?" "Three and Two"
New England Sampler: "I Dream of Doubloons"
New Voices: "The Hitchhiker"
Northern New England Review: "Biking Remembered," "End," "The Willey House Disaster in the Words of Lucy Crawford," "The Year We Fell in Love"
Our Places (chapbook): "Autumn Dusk Beside the River," "'Ktaadn': the Premiere," "Melancholy"
Potato Eyes: "Elegy to Logging"
Private Places (anthology): "Mount Mansfield, Age Eight"

Pudding: "Palm Sunday, San Pedro Sula"
San Fernandino Poetry Journal: "Renewal Reminds Me of the End"
Separate Doors: "Spring at Town Hall Bridge"
Slant: "Sometimes It's Luck"
Snow Apple: "As You Lie in the Hospital"
Stone Country: "This Weather Is No Womb"
Vermont Medicine: "Mary Fletcher Hospital, 1958"
Vital Signs (anthology): "We Travel North"

"Cases" was read by Garrison Keillor on *The Writer's Almanac*.

I am grateful beyond measure for the creative acuity of two individuals who assisted me in completing this book: my editor, Rennie McQuilkin, and my eldest son, Peter Towle.

TABLE OF CONTENTS

I. THIS BLADE OF LIFE

Biking Remembered / 15
The Year We Fell in Love / 17
One-on-One / 19
Your Faults, My Dear / 20
A Long Back Pack / 22
We Travel North / 24
Passage by Canoe / 25
Old Friends / 27
Fantasy / 28
Love Poem / 29
Green Mountain Solo / 30

II. TO HAVE SEEN THE CHILDREN

Sometimes It's Luck / 33
The Hitchhiker / 34
The Drive to Putnamville / 35
Wedding in the Underworld / 40
Generation / 41
Speck Pond's Light / 42
One Night Late Fall / 43
To the Boy with the Flying Hair / 44
End / 46
Honduran Mission / 48
Palm Sunday, San Pedro Sula / 49

TABLE OF CONTENTS

III. CONSTANT ENCOUNTERS WITH THE IMPOSSIBLE

A Young Boy Ponders His Death / 53
Three and Two / 54
Mary Fletcher Hospital, 1958 / 55
As You Lie in the Hospital / 57
Cases / 59
Requiem for a Marine and His Mate / 61
Buck / 63
What's It Like? / 65
Centenarian / 66
Dusk, a Stream, and a White Owl Cigar / 67
To a Friend Who Loves Trucks / 69
Elegy for Taylor / 70
A Drowning / 72
The Willey House Disaster in the Words of Lucy Crawford / 73
At the Hiroshima Hospital / 75
Renewal Reminds Me of the End / 76
The Architecture of Nine-Eleven / 77
Hooking Rugs and Ice-Fishing / 78
Variations on a Riff by Eubie Blake, Dead Age 100, 1984 / 80
Melancholy / 81

IV. A JOY GRUMLING UP

I Dream of Doubloons / 85
The Incredible / 86

TABLE OF CONTENTS

Mango and the Moon / 87
Footprints / 89
Elegy to Logging / 90
Spring at Town Hall Bridge / 92
Autumn Dusk Beside the River / 93
Mount Mansfield, Age Eight / 94
Katahdin, the People / 96
"Ktaadn": the Premiere / 97
Elegy for a Friend Who Climbed Mountains / 99
Madison Gulf / 100
At Bosebuck Mountain Camps / 102
Windblown Mountain Pond / 103
This Weather Is No Womb / 104

V. NOTES / 107

VI. ABOUT THE AUTHOR / 111

This Weather Is No Womb

I. This Blade of Life

Biking Remembered

That first one had narrow tires. Dad held the seat.
Off I went down the maple-lined street.
The first breath of freedom drew into my mouth.

The next year I got the balloon-tired Schwinn,
Wide handle bars and a Worcester Telegram
Route. Balance mastered, six mornings a week

I learned the meaning of dawn and cold, till
Vacation, the strain of hours uphill,
The exhilaration coasting down, the cramps

Of the long road and the rewards of gaining its end.
Endurance, sure, but the logbook of youth filled
After school on John's Evening Gazette route:

A daily conversation of spinning sprockets,
Flying papers, shouts, and jousts, experiments
Of flight over curbs and mounds,

Down lawns, through trees and brush. The bikes
Rarely broke, even on full speed leaps
To overhead limbs or piles of fallen leaves.

We rode railroad beds, dirt roads and ditches.
We raced no hands, double, down steep mogulled
Lanes; chased girls and every lower animal

Species. Nothing held us back. Dust
And grass stains, grime and breathless glee shot us
Clear through those years until

Girls caught us unprepared, tore us unawares from
Our wheeled steeds. We ate the apple of the future,
Clicked into the numbered shackles of sport,

Opened books, kissed the girls and
Put away the bicycles, our cult of speed,
Went to work, married, had kids and

Bought them...skinny-tired bikes.

The Year We Fell in Love

At age fifteen you could
masquerade as a boy. For winning
the D.A.R. prize you rose on Memorial Day
and orated the Gettysburg Address before
the monument of the dead. We were so
proud. Later, your little brother

brought home a stray dog. When
your aproned mother paced
the kitchen floor and you
defended the boy, your father beat
a tactical retreat to the game room.
I remember his body-builder's physique;

I was fat and short. But in the most
important picture my father ever took of me
the basketball is just above my sky-stretched
fingertips, feet off the ground,
lay-up sure thing on our tottering
garage-hung backboard. And across

a neighbor's yard, out of sight
behind a sculpted hedge
your stately, smoldering home.
Your mother welcomed me in spite
of oily dirt I tracked from my driveway
across the pink rugs and mirrored floors.

You were asleep
or counting losses in your
bedroom fortress of dolls
as I settled at the grand
to improvise: *Ain't misbehavin',
savin' my love for you.*

One-on-one

Fertility flowers in her blood, gathers
like the folds of a sari. Visceral

heat seeps under his clothes, through
his fingertips and toes. Her vine

winds through his lattice yet
they never touch: improvisation

on two flutes, a long rhythmic line,
a minor third, cascading fourths. She shifts,

the edges of her mouth curl up, lips
swell in a smile. A blush

warms the air between them, they barely
breathe. A flash

burns the palms of his hands.
The drive is floodlit. They're playing

one-on-one – "Tick, tick, tick," a dribble
scuffs the street.

Your Faults, My Dear

That Philadelphia
accent, those soft blue
eyes, yes, on alert,
taking in the home room
missiles, apple splats
against the board.
Just when I was
getting used to you,
it was summer, and you
were gone, then back,
browner and thinner,
smoother, but not
for me. The older,
taller boys saw
something. All
that body wanted
was babies.

Never saw that torso,
high beam or low, in any
magazine, but you've
swerved a few rigs, big ones.

All those babies and no
money. All those beds,
apartments, bungalows,
a sewing machine and cherry table

bought on time. All that
crying, those diaper pails,
top hat and tails, "taking
a chance on...."
whatever it is.

Make a man seem small,
bringing those red heads
into the world head first,
occiput posterior.
Make a man
want to cry.

A Long Back Pack

It was not so much the puzzle of the way
through logging slash, the stop and search,
heft pack and start again; nor the heat dripping,
nor you, really, in tears having started
a wrong direction into brambles and flood rubble
(our trail on the map had long dimmed
to moose and deer tracks). We were
slipping apart, today, on the Fourth of July
in America, alone, pressing into a valley
beyond chainsaw and firecracker, miles
from any other person. In late sun we
lay down together on a grassy clearing
beside a stream crossing.

                        Next day
on our long climb up the stream bed
onto the bald ridge, we had barely gone
halfway by noon. A long traverse
and third peak lay ahead. By then
we weren't lost but lagged. I felt
as if my face were sliding off,
the only thing that held me together,
the dirt and sweat of my body.
We raged against each other,
and ground behind the last mountain
into a deserted lean-to. Strain
slipped off with the packs. At the stream,

amazing, your naked body turned a waterfall
upside down. We lathered off grime
and soothed our scrapes. You
made up your face.

A stove roar under splash
of rain on the corrugated roof drifted us
toward sleep.

Next morning we rose to mount
the last peak, a hope-draining stretch
over boulder, root and granite slab,
but beyond the summit we eased down pine needle
and gravel slope to the car and camp,
and embraced in a pond, it seemed for hours,
until three days' heat drifted away
like a fragment of leaf.

We Travel North

Berlin, New Hampshire, midwinter,
we drive the tight, pot-holed streets.
Smog that smells like cabbage rot
rises from the pulp-encrusted mill
across the frothy Androscoggin.

I grasp your hand. Above the mill
log ramparts jut in the stream
now black and cleaned; we follow north,
wind along sways of the river,
backwaters frozen tight.

Alertness grows. As the river thins
you snuggle in the low-blowing cloud,
sun-edged, toward the long climb high
to Dixville Notch. Puffs of snow
pulsate, billow, nudge our course.

Higher up we lurch, wild-eyed, climb
higher — snow gusts swirl between
black-faced cliffs, crystals flare.
We peak the brim, weightless, weak,
then coast around the Balsam pool.

Our pace uncoils, releases down
new watershed. Chimney smoke
wavers and dissipates above,
while below this arctic plain
seeds of trees and water wait.

Passage by Canoe

It could have been an elm skeleton
eroded from a bank of the upper Connecticut,
floating to this narrow turn ten feet deep
and swift, hung up by its limbs, like an iceberg
mostly under water bisecting the flow, yet
drawing it
                to itself as if sucking water
from root tips to branching arms pointing
downstream like a drowning man or a Bedouin
in quicksand, one hand visible, twitching,
pleading for air.
                    In this near flood stage,
late spring, we were being lofted from beneath
more than ruddering the canoe. As we
approached the tree, one of us said left
by the sandbar, the other, right
on the peripheral curve. Broadsided between
two ideas, we were drawn up and
transfixed on the jutting limb. We tipped
eccentrically and filled with raw snow melt.

"Swim to the sand bar," I pleaded twice.
She launched off, whooping in the frigid pour,
thrashing sparks in the river bend. I
jockeyed the hull off the slimy limb,
submarined it under another branch and
eased its royal waterloggedness
to the sand bar farther down.

Paddles and pack unlashed, we stripped
to wring out and dry in a hazy sun, to
the distant grind of a tractor across
floodplain fields of corn.

Cast off, we meandered by ducks
diving in shallows, quarreling kingfishers,
the whir and sweep of swallows. In a wide
and gentle whirlpool miles down the river,
we dipped our paddles deep for the last time,
swung to shore, two weathered
salts in an old green canoe.

Old Friends

They dream of waterfalls in the wood,
Couples dancing to the fiddle's whine,
Storefronts filled with loaves of bread,
Old men and women lifting wine

To each others' lips to taste their long
And lovely lives together. They stand,
Arm in arm and gather horizon's
Sun setting beyond the rippled land

Where they have labored this whole day
And now will shuffle back to bed
And rest with gratitude for this blade
Of life cut into the soil of death,

As they have savored salt and sipped
The spring's cool bubble at their lips.

Fantasy

I look
at the hills
that billow from the sea
and I see
an old woman
stroke her husband's cheek
as he dozes
in the open
air
and a young girl
brush long russet hair
pirouette
and wave it
high over walls
that weave like a net
in rippled folds
back
to the sea.

Love Poem

After I woke you from the bed of youth
with piano notes of morning sun
and hurdled between my adolescence
and your unqualified smile,

we climbed the powdery hill
and tobogganed to a first embrace,
lay naked on ochre sand
in saffron, wind-fluttered sun,

wept behind the windows
of our longing….and reared
the children: the red-bearded bear,
the fierce-muscled lamb.

Today you stand here circled
by mountain's rippled line;
poplar leaves flash and fall
silent on our common ground.

Green Mountain Solo

Mist, heavy cream spreads
over a pasture of grazing cows.

Fantasies of you warble in my head
like the thrush's song. Toad's feet
and mine slide in the black soil as

downhill tingles of swamp and bracken
replace aromas of evergreen and bare rock
just passed. The rustle of chipmunks,
I think, could be your footsteps.

Seated by a stream I blend
an orange salamander
with rusty sprigs of dead spruce
the colors of our children's hair.

Further on, small white butterflies burst up
and scatter like confetti on the trail.
Indeed, I end this fortunate passage, as
after a wedding feast. I dream – today

our first grandchild, a perfect boy
will be born. No rain dampens
the premonition. I climb and then

descend in the rhythm of easy
swings to breathe with you again.

II. To Have Seen the Children

Sometimes It's Luck

You were buoyant as a polar bear cub
when we capsized in heavy current
over a submerged log. Drawn under,
you hung on and grappled up
for air. You did not drift

away. Now, full man, you lead
and clear the way in a mountain rescue.
I follow on the stretcher lunging
back to that year you clung
while I leaped to save the canoe. Further

back when you were three, you bubbled
down in a pool when I was turned away.
Soon enough I whirled around,
dove, and flung you on the edge. Sometimes
it's luck or God. We live at the rim

of the spun world. In the labor
of birth your head would not pass
the pelvic ring. For years I heard
the rush of bottled blood,
the thud of swinging doors,

no news. You waited
for a forceps turn, then
molded and crowned up pink
and fat, my rescuer,
lumped, and whole.

The Hitchhiker

The glue and tape from hiding cash
in shoes and pack were strewn among
torn maps and string, but the guide
for hitchhikers and sterno stove were gone:
bored with summer work, not quite sixteen,
with my blessing, my son left home.

Each telephone ring struck fear and hope.
"Have you heard?" she asked. "No word, none."
The call came from Biloxi – "on the way to Mexico."
I had to cheer the daylight of his voice,
but relief seeped away as the sun set;
insects fluttered and popped in the lampshades,
cats stretched and sharpened their claws on the walls.

By the call from Corpus Christi for a plane ticket
my brain sputtered in blue flame.
Restore his body, Christ, to this house;
fill these fitful rooms with his breath.
At a late call I raged to the airport.
In the empty lobby, "Am I forsaken?"
From nowhere, he ran up with a wave and a smile.
Freer than before, I hugged him tighter.

The Drive to Putnamville

The route out of the city is streaked with ice
and dusted between the tire lines
with new snow.

       Plowed, it buries
the guard rails along the steep side hill
that bends me north.

          The afternoon is lighted
flat, no sun, seeping cold. White earth
drifts to the farmhouse sills. Livestock

chew and snort in the barns. Are you safe, son,
in this country, deep in cold? The land rises
along a stream that snaps the road

            like a bullwhip.
Blanched fields shift to clouds of winter woods.
I have been to your cabin once a year ago;

have I seen you since?
Corn and beans have been planted, tended,
brought in, and now

       the ground is firm again.
Where do I turn off to your shack? Serkin plays
Beethoven on the radio. The land seems strange:

more houses, wisps of smoke, almost dusk. Here's
Putnamville – I must have passed your dirt road.
Cars stand

        running at the two-pump
country store, lights are on
but your car's not here.

               Fifty cents for
coffee in a Styrofoam cup. I ask
only in my head the way to your shack,

afraid to inquire if you've been about:
"You know, the big red-head with the bushy beard,
old shaggy clothes,

            the dancing man with guitar,
soft smiley voice?" A man pumps gas, shivers
and stamps, says nothing.

I continue north, search
the yards of homes I pass for your
small gray car. They could be friends,

you could have stopped to visit. No sign
at the Post Office, none
at the store.

                Coffee's
gone, I turn around, afraid for no
obvious reason. Back past the gas pumps

now, there's only one left turn over the stream – it
must be yours. It passes east then north by farms
and into the woods.

                              Is this the way? The road
ruts by a mailbox: *Towle,* in crude green. Old cars
nearby are mounds of snow. I stop

                                    and get out.
Iced tracks pull me over the small rise to the flapping
plastic-covered porch door. Oil cans,

firewood on the porch are frosted
blocks of ice. I swing open your insulation-
silvered door

                      and enter your body, warm,
orderly, wood chunks smoldering in the stove; piles
of books, tapes, straggly plants,

a mat for meditation on the floor. Speak,
son. Up the ladder, no breathing, the loft is empty.
I can almost smell you but

there's no one
here. I check the wood shed, the door sticks
half open, no one inside. No foot prints track

into the woods. You're off, but why
do I feel you here in this hut, in these woods,
over these fields?

    Missing you, son,
I imagine no good, find no metaphor
that comforts.

    You are flying everywhere,
through the dead-leafed oak trees cracking
cold.

   The sun has set, I shiver. You sail off,
the warm cocoon of house around you, then circle back
oblivious.

    "Hi Dad," I imagine you might say
in your tentative tenor. Instead, I step outside,
round the path, climb in my car

       and all
I hear is Coltrane and Vivaldi. No sure flesh.
You're *On the Road to Freedom,* I've heard you sing,

but where? Please give me a sign, son; step out
from behind each of these trees beside the road,
burst up

        through this crust of snow. I worm
back into the city. Its old patrician frames
are frosted, too, like blocks of ice.

Their window eyes beam heat into this absolute
and isolate dark
without you.

Wedding in the Underworld

You may never see such a celebration as this,
at least not in a church. Streamers leap out of the hands of
dancers like steel flames and flutter over the crowd.
Joyous Easter choruses roll obscenely through the tabernacle.

There aren't enough chairs. Plenty of horns for a wedding,
tubas and bones, and a plethora of piccolos, oboes, and flutes.
The father of the groom brings in chairs from down below
for all the unknown faces in the vestibule, but the music stands

break, and he, all decorum, is desiccated to smoke.
His son is being conveyed like Cleopatra on an Elizabethan stage,
on a wheeled platform like a mechanic's creeper, along the edge
of a churning stream. It is poisoned, putrid, and vile; three headed

Cerberus blocks his way. Now it clears. The bridegroom
bends down but hesitates, scared out of his wits! Never mind,
he rolls to the edge, leans over ... and sips. Right there
high up one trumpet blares, like the drone of a bagpipe,

and the blond, pony-tailed bride enters the room.

Generation

Your grandmother questions my grasp sometimes
as I whirl through the house, you
cradled in one arm. You won't remember,
but I've got you by one thigh bone, firm

as a hand hold on a rock climb.
I delivered seventy-five babies like you
when I was an intern. One came so fast
the nurse was closer and did it

with her bare hands. Each head all wet
and slippery slid into the room; we cleared
the mouth and nose and let air in. One firm
hand circling the neck, the shoulders and body

came easier than a fish. The other hand held
one solid leg or two. We never let a baby fall,
no matter what. King of a lesser tummy,
we laid you down atop your mother's world.

Speck Pond's Light

You, woman, my last born
sunning on a boulder,
yesterday were the pulse and swing
between Mahoosuc and Fulling Mills cliffs.

As you spanned chasms, hand holds
on roots, the dark
rasped and gurgled.

Today, on a granite floor direct sun
flares our slab up to the basin pond
and lights your face as we
sit and talk on the brim.

Abruptly, a robber jay starts
to fret and ground squirrels
halt their scurrying. With a hum
a ruling hawk flutters in and lights
on a branch dangling close
to your boulder sun.

Last night that same sun
fired the full moon's rise
above the water. Candle lamp swinging,
we stumbled around shore on a stony
tightrope to the outlet of the pond,
an edge of earth.

One Night Late Fall

Black bear, sleek and sure
that eats our berries,
I don't see you but you're there
and you'll be back.

Shadowed doe, plump with summer,
drift into moonlight on the lawn,
escape the hunter's gun
to graze our frosted grass
and saunter off.

My children gone,
this room is dark,
the woodstove sputters
flame across the floor.

To the Boy with the Flying Hair

Not even one year old
how can you know
as you crawl, smiling
through a field of flaming
Devil's Paintbrushes,

I look behind you
to your father, a little boy
standing sentry still,
one hand gently circling my knee,
the other pulling his ear,
wide-eyed, watching with me
as his older brother, maybe five,
darts back and forth
to dodge oncoming crowds
of people on the sidewalk.

At first I think he's panicked,
searching for us, being swept
as if toward a storm drain.
Your father grips me a little
tighter.
        But the sun is shining.
Big brother shifts and dances
in pure play, oblivious,
certain your father has me

safely anchored with his soft arm,
transfixed as I am now
by your steady smile
and sunburst, wild flying hair.

End

Last game, you started,
right defensive end, a sky-diver
descended on the field at halftime
and in the third quarter you appeared
in the blue backfield in a running
duel with the quarterback. In a flurry
of arms, spider and fly, yours stuck,
first one hand, then full clasp
and you melted together into the
ragged turf. A game for the defense
you won, seven to two.

After hard loss earlier
that year you walked through rain
and tears to the lockers. Further
back in your last high school game
Thanksgiving mud froze numbers and
Colors in a double O tie.

Then back the year before, at home
in the sun keying a halfback
alone in their backfield you speared
a drop-back pass, clean interception
high overhead, and ran untouched,
an easy arc, then long stiff stride
to the only score of the day.

The crowd has filtered down but I stay
against the top rail of the stands, sun
settling into the trees beyond
the athletic fields. You're still
loitering out on the field, shirt off,
helmet lolling sideways on the chalk.
Your kid brother, the manager, rolls
or unrolls tape on some limb or other
in a tangle of torn pads. Your face
is stunned in grit and grass stain.
The goal posts dim into the dark.

Honduran Mission

Brown baby,
three years old, rod legs,
knob knees, big dry eyes aim
"recto" up to me.

One bony hand grasps
a frayed shelf. Bloated belly thrusts,
and flat, mud-encrusted feet blend
into the ground. Six brothers and sisters

peer around, a little less moribund. Weeping
heat flows through the narrow passage
between the shacks. Nothing
moves but haze and dogs, dirty

as the children. A stone stove
smokes the rancid air; on its top
tortillas coagulate the fumes.
I've never felt so watched.

Palm Sunday, San Pedro Sula

Malarial shakes and dysenteric
blood loss stain
the countryside. The bulbous-bellied
and stick-limb Kwashiorkor brood
ride out of the jungle on the backs

of donkeys. At road blocks
and on city streets soldiers
wave automatic rifles with 7-UP
decals on their stocks.
The guns are loaded.

     Children
in starched dress clothes
march behind the statue
of Christ on a donkey
borne on the elders' shoulders,
and sing hosanna.

     Tightened
fists open out under the donkey's hooves
and Christ floats
through waving palms to the cathedral.
When the priest in white robes
high on the balcony
splashes water from the font, squeals

rise from the crowd. Tears
run down the youthful faces.

Laughter and weeping sound
the same in any language.

To have seen the children was enough.

III. Constant Encounters with the Impossible

A Young Boy Ponders his Death

Those flapping wings, snaps and rustles
in the bush are hawks with claws that tear
and make you bleed. Beware. If I climb
that pleading oak that stabs to their nest,
they will cry and slash. I may lose
an eye, weep down the limbs and soak
into the sandy soil.
                    Where no air flows,
grandfather, do worms crawl, do I need
to die to join you by the roots
and rivulets in the ground, or —
will you return in mid-winter cold:
sweet skin, thin frame, grease-stained clothes,
and bark at the door with a high
"raf, raf, raf," as you always did,
absurd and happy man? And then,
                                will I hug
those grimy Blue Sunoco trousers
to leave mother and father in the comfort
of the kerosene range and go back
with you into the snow?
                        Stark eye,
surround me in earth wings, hold me,
keep me warm and when it's time
clamp me in talons and soar
above breath into the sun.

Three and Two

He bothered no one,
sitting on an elm log
that said *No
Trespassing* on a rusting
sideways sign.

Mosquitos zig-zagged
about his head in rhythm
to the hum of trucks
down Route 10 across
the bridge. His shadow

shot out twenty feet.
Blown ash leaves turned
a supernatural shine
in horizontal light.
He grew longer, even

as the light failed,
and he was gone. The dusk
spread west in broad
strokes, palming the river lows
and molding the hills.

It stroked him as
the late inning stopper rubs
a last new ball, fingers
the stitches of the mountain
ridge, and throws.

Mary Fletcher Hospital, 1958

Deep cold. Late at night
the ward is dim. Cousin, like kid-sister,
in the starched gray dress of a student nurse,
you stand behind the low desk, phone in hand,
flushed, looking out
over the double row of beds. My white-buck
soles creak down the polished floor,
palpating the tile like a native
on the hunt. I breathe out through my
teeth, just another student,
third year medical, starched white,
and green.
                We were it, 2:00 a.m., intern,
resident in bed, charge nurse down the other hall.

A woman, dusky as the ward, breathes deeply,
bubbles froth at her lips. "Let's turn up
the oxygen," I say, for want of something
more clever. You speak blood pressure and pulse.
Her eyes seem to turn inward, searching
for breath. We tip up the head of her bed,
you suction her mouth. She turns her head
to you in gratitude and lowers her lids
over vacant eyes.
                The room becomes
silent but for a chorus
of hushed breathing. Wind
whines through cracks in the window frames. Snow

brushes the glass. One hand in mine,
one in yours, she quiets
and goes to sleep.

As You Lie in the Hospital

A light squall provokes the ripple
in front of my feet. This May afternoon's
not hot but green on the skin of fish.
Leaves are pure, inviolate.
See? A gust turns them back
yellow, as that sheet of clear
run-off ignites the stone mosaic
beneath. The almost impossible flow
over the earth reminds me
                            that I
have glided so effortlessly down
a mountain trail, I barely touched
a rock, a patch of dirt, never
really secured land until
I floated just millimeters
off the earth. Impossible? Perhaps,
but it has happened and not in a dream.

We are not tethered completely
to the earth. Icarus went too high.
If we can leave earth down a slope
for one second, why not two or three
or more? Quantum theory states
all things are not just being, rather,
happening.
               My friend, you float over
this river. You always will. I clomp

down midstream, boots clutching
the rock, a staff in either hand
to hold my spine erect against
the current pressing against the deep.

Cases

Man comes in to Emergency with loss
of vision in one eye, works full-time,
in his sixties. It goes away and he wants
to go home. Internist and eye doctor
find nothing. I find something and say,

No. Family says I'm over-
reacting but they all agree, reluctantly.
Urgent angiogram – surgery on the neck arteries
is booked for the following morning. That night
his opposite side becomes paralyzed.

Emergency surgery cleans out a nearly
blocked vessel. They don't appreciate the
post-operative pain. They don't appreciate
my style or anything about me. He *walks out*
saved from an almost certain

permanent disability. A man comes in,
in his sixties, can't work, losing weight,
muscles are twitching, hard to swallow,
hard to talk. Do some tests,
tell his wife and him he's got

Lou Gehrig's Disease, it will affect his
breathing, he's going to die, it will be
tough, we'll try some things. We do,

he gets worse, can't walk, can't feed
himself. I visit the house: a small

cape with a screened porch behind
a variety store in a small town in
New Hampshire. He gets worse, I visit
some more, talk some to him,
to his wife and son, he dies.

Requiem for a Marine and his Mate

For all the shrimp they could eat,
a dollar a bucket, steamed
tender in ocean brine

she opened her lips
and he fed her more
than she had hoped

and in return she raised
red wine to his waiting mouth.
They roamed the Mayport dunes

that summer, nineteen forty-one.
From other beaches on Tarawa,
Iwo, Guam he did not quite

return. Now after forty years
huge steaming plates
of crab legs are piled like kindling.

Our fingers, wrinkled in the fray,
heap up the shells like flames.
He died by his own hand

that once had fed her, a death from war
that charred but could not
draw her body down, until antiquity

folded her into her birth ground,
Alabama. I tease a long pink
strip of crab leg before your lips

and pop it in. We each swallow
a long draught, four lives deep,
two lovers gone.

Buck

Cockeyed speculation, his old lady called it
when he said in his next life he'd return
as a deer. "Young buck with a big rack
of horns?" she smirked. He grumbled a deep cough,
shuffled out with the care arthritic limbs demand
and stepped off the deck. Inside, later
a chill hovered. He grabbed the shirt
over his heart and twisted. Pulseless
he slumped to the floor like the bags of potatoes
he'd stacked his whole life, wrinkled and soft
as the last sack in spring ready to split and seed.

The death simmered down, people went home
and she settled back in the house by the pond.
"I miss the old guy to haul wood. By Jesus,
this house leaks as bad as a pail left
two years on a stump." She was warmest
in the upstairs bedroom, heat rising
from the kitchen below. Sun once in a while
beamed through the dormer that looked
at night like a one eyed fool winking
over the lake at those "ice fishing idiots,"
she, alone, stitching on a quilt.

One night she's about to snap off the light.
"Clomp, clomp" on the deck, so she flips the switch
and gazes down on the boards streaked with moon

reflected off the snow. The buck looks through
the glass dining room doors, wood stove
cracking red flame around its draft. *Damn.*
He turns by the kitchen door, makes
a feeble, clumsy hop on the steps and ambles
down the shoreline, picking his way,
an old man, head high, half blind
and hungry, out for fresh air and a smoke.

What's It Like?

You made it, Mother, antiquity – you've
left old age behind. Your memory so refined
and huge has squeezed anticipation down
to dust on the floor. Inscrutable
abandon romps like ponies in a ring
around your hair. Your body folds down
closer to the earth. Your doubts endure;
I adore their hiding places, take them
with the certainties – a bargain to me,
no apologies needed. You do not shrink.
You round up like a stone, long
in a stream bed. In spring
the run-off from the mountain peaks
warms the river valley where you live,
far from the crags where you once faced
into the spires of weather.

Centenarian

Vegetables ripen in the sun
even without enough manure.
The grass is warm. You survive,
mother. I dearly hope this sun
blanches the pain out of your back
and limbs. You endure because
you expect no other way.
Faith is your lesson to us.
I take grief into my gut
day after day until I am
intoxicated with your life.
You are not impressed. Action
is your poetry and it writes
itself every time you take
a breath. Neither work nor love is
enough. Power is the cycle of the planets,
and the shining of this summer sun.
You suffer but do not speak. I am
less than a knot on the visor of your cap,
a crack on the lip of your cup.
Only my genes can save me.

Dusk, a Stream, and a White Owl Cigar

A purple-crested duck
wallows in the bouldered rush. Now
it mounts a wet stone, peers
in the brush along the shore,
and launches off upstream, turns
and flies a determined line down
and gone. A deer will
soon appear to drink.

This coffee's cooling fast.
I'm a grandfather twice. I roll my
suitcoat collar up and button it.
Four springs ago this month
mother was dying. When she knew
father would be cared for, she perished.
I begin to shiver. Smoke
burns out my fingers. The pen jerks
in my hand. This swirl could be
the subway tube, a turnstyle,
but it's the Swift turned up full,
zagging in front of me, inches
from my numbing toes. I flick
ashes on the whirlpool – bubbling mix
of a life, sanded down.

When did she realize she was

getting old, that she was not
the smooth rock but the stream
curving over it, when were too many
glistening tufts like silk
clouding the setting sun? Smoke spreads
over the damp motion of the waves,
swings, darts and dissolves away.

My stiffened fingers
burn on the stub. I fling it
in rippling sky, float out with one
perfect orange maple leaf. Not her, me.

To a Friend Who Loves Trucks

I have just read a book by Weldon Kees,
dark poems we could not hope to brighten.
He died in a fall of self-intent,
we assume, from his disappearance and his car
found near the Golden Gate Bridge.

What next? Eighteen wheelers swing
into my brain. Might they burst
upon you in that executive suite
at Bethlehem Steel? Can you
double-clutch down through
the gears, air brakes screaming
over the bay, stop, and drag him
into the cab off the bridge's rail?

He's gone. But I cannot leave him
no matter how deep, and I don't have
the strength to dredge him up. I need
your help, lover of winches, coal mines,
and trucks. I cannot bear the leap,
the pulsing rush of air, the strike.

Elegy for Taylor

The man was a genius
but, he said, all people are geniuses.
We had thought he had another life,
but all the time he was giving his future away.
Care for patients was his trope of creation.

He loved his family and his friends
but could be a lonely man at his computer,
his artifacts cluttered around him.
Without trying he built a legend out of words.
He was shy. Abstraction made him uneasy.
His only resort was example,
and the metaphor. He could perplex himself
with his own precision of thought.

But he purified the landscape
of expression and imitated no one,
mandated us to do likewise, not imitate him.
Such would be, of course, impossible.
He would say, *Live your best self,*
you will never die, but he would say it better.

He was a north country saint
folded over the counter at the nurse's station
scribbling notes, attempting to heal where science
would not dare venture, in a constant encounter
with the impossible.

He was a quiet man. When exasperated, still
he was deeply amused by his fellows.
He gave his love away. It limped out the door
but never faltered, shuffled down
Main Street on two Canadian crutches.
It has not failed. It has not passed away.

A Drowning

He was skating in the depth of winter, temperature
way below zero, bob houses poised
like Buddhist monks on the lake. You know
how big our lake is, how it becomes
a byway of commerce in the summer. Far
out I hear the bite of blade, scraping
on patches of clear glare, ripples of waves
arrested in ice, and pool-like circles
of wind-packed snow on the surface.

Two hours from here, ten miles up
where they found him, a warm spring had
thinned the ice. He perished
alone, weighted by his gleaming blades.
No struggle, there wasn't time. He was
singing out loud, chopping the air
with his arms, flying, when an edge caught in
slush and the mouth of death swallowed him.

In spring the divers recovered his body, we
buried him in the town cemetery. Wind
gusts across the water, osprey
soar and dive, hulls toss and spray.
That was twenty years ago.

The Willey House Disaster
in the Words of Lucy Crawford

The summer was dry and hot.
August twenty-seventh
at four a.m. it began to rain.
Brooks and rivers rose,
fed from the peaks, and winds
spilled water like streams through the air.
Thunder cracked over the ridges
and the roots of spruce trees
and scrub loosed their hold.
The heights split, sheared off
their walls and began to slide.

A tree two feet across
plunged, roots first, into the back
of the barn, pinned a cow in her stall,
udder full of milk.
One cataract of gravel, brush
and rock poured toward the house;
boulders splintered, trees
heaved through the air and a different thunder
rumbled into the valleys.
The deafened family had rushed out
to a refuge near the house but the dark,
darker than night came down.

At dusk a stranger on foot

found the house untouched,
rubble parted to either side.
Inside, bed clothes were ruffled,
and dinner dishes lay
unbroken on the table. Out
in the barn he loosed the cow
from a crumpled stall. Two horses
impaled, lay dead. He ate,
fed a whining dog, and slept.

Next day flies attended
a pile of floodwood. They found
the parents and one child buried,
and the eldest daughter
twelve years old, across
the swollen river, no bruise or mark,
fair and pleasant, drowned.
Three children still lie in the notch.

I fashioned a sign,
"The Family Found Here,"
and nailed it to a dead tree.
Some of the occupants since that time
worse than brutes
tore it down, used it for fuel.

At the Hiroshima Hospital

a couple holding their newborn child
steps out the front door held
open by a nurse   she smiles

in delivery a man holds his wife as
their son is born and the doctor
raises the infant to their eyes

down the hall a woman's
breath quickens a contraction
builds she cannot help pushing

flash at the door   the round
infant wrapped in fluff and bonnet sucks
out of its mother's arms and sweeps down

the street
rumbling   the doctor
pitches back   the floor

folds   a cry
never comes   mushroom cloud
crowns

Renewal Reminds Me of the End

Flecks of song birds spatter the yard.
Heat careens in ape-like strides
scouring the corridors of the house.

Our marrow has been sucked clean
by nuclear fission.
The lines in our hands whiten.

Mercy says no,
no neighbors appear. The sun
domineers and we are not here.

The world is a gallows.
The hangman burns beside the corpse.
Crows twitch in the dust.

The vulture's beak bleeds
and the sewer rat floats
encrusted to a tepid sea.

The Architecture of Nine-Eleven

Forty-five minutes after the twin towers
of the World Trade Center collapsed,
his class on modern architecture convened
at Yale: undergraduates, graduate
students, adult auditors. Some doubted
he would appear. The great professor, at least
five times retired until now they just let him
go on as he would into his late eighties, stood
beside the podium and said that some
would question the decorum of holding a class
in the face of such a tragedy but he said:

"We are here to study man's creation,
the human reach for greatness, unbounded
optimism, ingenuity with the products
of our skill and labor. We will not allow
the destroyer to prevail." He discussed
the brilliance of the conception and construction.
In so short a time he had gathered
a retrospective of drawings and lantern slides.
He was as incisive and original as ever. When
about fifteen minutes of class remained,
he concluded. A pause, he bowed, he wept.

Hooking Rugs and Ice-Fishing

He volunteered with a dying patient
expecting to go through the five stages of grief
at the first meeting. Instead
she talked about hooking rugs:

the needle, the thread, the cloth,
the rhythmic movement of the hands.
He tried other matters in conversation —
she talked of hooking rugs.

On the next visit she spoke of the intricacies
and hardships of ice-fishing that her husband
had done before his death. Week after week,
hooking rugs and ice-fishing.

Angered, he said to friends,
"I can't go on with this
interminable hooking rugs
and ice-fishing."

One day as they sat
in the hospital cafeteria,
she going on, he bored and vexed
with hooking rugs and ice-fishing

the room
went silent, air turned

a luminous shade of green, hooking
rugs and ice

fishing stopped. She leaned over and said
"I could not have done this
without you,"
then on again with hooking rugs

and ice-fishing. Soon after, she died. At the funeral

relatives said to him, "Thank you —
all she ever spoke about
was you."

Variations on a Riff by Eubie Blake, Dead Age 100, 1984

Be grateful for luck
        My daughter in tights, playful
                This drunken Thanksgiving
                Could have been worse, someone
        Moody and complex
                Could have died
Pay the thunder no mind
        Her mother's tears surface today
                I have no quarrel with failure except
        With no one to wipe them
        They drip on the sand
                Failure of the heart
Listen to the birds
        I know I'm growing old, grandma said
                MRI pictures are so beautiful
        When I try
        To climb trees
                And no one understands why
And don't hate nobody
        On her last day she said
                "Legislation is helpless against"
        Give him a stiff drink
                "The wild prayer of longing"

Melancholy

Why does sadness settle over so much
        joyous and beautiful life,
as if a giant beaver family has dammed
        every stream and made
the north woods a perpetual bog, so wet
        birch bark will barely light?

We do not wish Bull's Blood wine to pass
        its prime not drunk, we need not
be lonely in our separate quests, nor blind
        nor timid, nor faint of heart.
Just now a loon calls for an absent mate,
        night chill sparkles in the sky,
I feel the scary power of words – the books
        pile up, some of them banned.

The sad parade is nonetheless
        full of color and dancing children.
Without the melancholy we would be
        bedazzled by the light.

IV. A Joy Grumbling Up

I Dream of Doubloons

There is a time before dawn
as the blot of night eases,
ocean ripples calm,
and the stars' brightness dulls
when the islands off shore are perfectly black
and the clouds above,
not airy mist, are
lions, horses, Poseidon.

I dream of doubloons, Dead Man's Chest,
the painful whiteness of sand at noon,
the wind that rattles shutters
hour after hour and now
explosive calm
save brush of breakers on the beach,
creaks and cheeps in the bush
and beyond, the cock's crow.

The Incredible

dawn casts the islands
tangerine, the sea
moves toward us in wind
ripples as from a hidden
wheel east of a far isle's
bay, a flickering
fans before us from a rim
of coal that animates
the mist. There's
water in the air, green
and purple cloud. Guana's
on fire, spreading to Gorda
and Anegada; flames
streak in bands behind
cloud smoke. We
squint to shun the heat
that rolls in day.

Mango and the Moon

Mango,
gray and black
squints off,
listens to this
or that or thinks about
being alone now, his woman
drunk, fallen in the fire, to be
in hospital a few more weeks. "I drunk two
bottles of Cruzan rum a night in my day. Gave
it up. I still did long day's work but it was no
more good for me. Just quit
right off. She must too.
Yes, just quit."
Quiet, thin,
the moon
grays
horizon cloud by
bedtime. From the patio
gas pilot glow makes the house
a theater set awaiting actors to
open the final act. Black cloud masses
ringed with silver advance over the house
blotting stars, then far shore
phosphoresces. A glistening hole
the size of a gap in the cloud
moves toward this chair,
the size of a skin

graft
from a thigh
across the span of water.
Quiet! It's touching the shore.
Glints of white are pacing up this hillside,
spears, lean legs, crystal fire,
a shimmering. Look up! A bowl!
Cratered dust has bloomed,
old tide-puller
soars.

Footprints

mark the fine red sand beside the trail: a man's
shoe, horse's hooves, a paw. Navajo
sandstone looms four hundred feet
to either side streaked white by sea stones,
not snow, striated like stacks of old coins
pocked as with claw prints of quaint
cretaceous birds.   A partridge flushes through
pale blue sage brush. Shadow strikes my face
like a blade of ice. The stone of
canyon wall abrades.   A chipmunk
leaves a puff of dust across my path. I turn
back through black volcanic caves, lose
my way for a moment, hum, "All
through the Night," over and over, hear
bubbling water deep beneath my feet,
enter my history, inscriptions
in the sand.

Elegy to Logging

Two rust-corroded
locomotives peer
from underbrush,
headlights gutted like
cyclopean eyes. Wheels
on tracks sink beneath
leaf-strewn turf. One cab
is stripped away, the other
heels farther than the dumping ramp
out on Chesuncook Lake. Foot-thick
tree trunks lean away
but nudge the black mass,
saplings search
through gaps.

Back before it begins its final tumbles
into the lake, interrupted once, perhaps,
generations back by fallen logs or a beaver dam,
Leadbetter Stream widens into deadwater and
a vast field of swamp grass. No stumps,
no driftwood, only shallows over
mud deeper than a paddle-plunge in a loose mesh
of long-stemmed green. Small dragon
flies hover and dart down, crackling
their wings on the grass. No long
hoofed legs break the breeze, no squirrel
squabble filters from the woods, no tree

thuds to the sun-patched ground. Listen:
a lap on the canoe's side,
a lip-break of paddle, a whisper
of hull on lily pads.

A sparrow's flutter and the faint breeze
stop, breath holds for a moment,
not even
drift.

Spring at Town Hall Bridge

Where winter stream arrests in ice
Water forges now in sheets,
A pulsing foamer and molder that bites
And licks the top of the bank, teases
Away pine needles and pieces of leaf.

Tongues of mist in morning air
Wave over the hiss and roar;
A man stands perfectly bare
In the middle of the chilled flow,
His body a pale cast of snow.

As yellow buds at stream edge open,
Round walls of sound crash,
Sparkle and flutter; and the surge rolls,
Sweeps its arm's urged flesh
To the plow point in warming earth.

Autumn Dusk beside the River

This shore of grass
        and weed
                browns in its
pale, long-limbed, brittle age,
        the grain
                delicate as
lace of finest unbleached
        thread, flaxen, bowed down
                to the warm
earth's loss. Under snow
        these secret seeds will wait
                to sing.
A joy will grumble up out of
        the soil into pure
                melody,
ring in the air, skip light
        in the morning
                sun.

Mount Mansfield, Age Eight

Part way through the night my feet
bound up in pain like a hawk's claws
after climbing the mountain with pack
and parents, sleeping chilled under
hard wool blankets on an iron cot
in the unheated basement
of the hotel under The Nose long
gone now to "expert trail" and
"warming hut." We cooked out
on the open ridge next morning
up toward The Chin, summit breeze fanning
the flaming sticks of scrub,
me in shorts, khaki sweater,
and Scout issue low-cut shoes,
the summer after Pearl Harbor, Dad too old
to be drafted, handsome as
a movie star, Mom, brave as any recruit.

We went on that day below
The Nose ledge through a musty cavern
of hanging moss and gnarled roots over
great sheets of granite rock, *so depthless-deep
and nebulous and dim.*

I had forgotten this
cool, damp cave until now
when I enter again — strange — aura

of deep solitude — another life — through
a passageway to an unknown
world that might be a thousand years, five
thousand years ago or might be
a thousand years hence, or five thousand.
Is this my Limbo, *the desolate chasm*
where rolls the thunder of Hell's eternal cry?
Poets emerge from the haze, God
having taken the saints into heaven.

Katahdin: the People

I feel a certain cordiality here,
committed to the mountain like
vows. The weather clears, sky
heavy with old memories from
the first youthful test, a foolish
climb up The Chimney.

With mother on the second trip we
approached her coming up to meet us
as we descended the Cathedral Trail,
our Sermon on the Mount.

                                  Then
you returned, again and again, around
the sacred circle – until you did not return
any more. Time passed.
You died. I began to return.
This time at Russell Pond
we have picked a pint of blueberries and
prepared for the summit haul, sixteen miles

in blowing cloud over North Peaks
to close the loop once more,
your son and I.

"Ktaadn": the Premiere

Wire-beard, you move through seated players
to the podium. Large man with the grace
of a bull moose, you loom to full height
and lift sixty instruments with your arms.
Beneath that rumpled jacket,
spinal muscle ripples and draws
as it did below the summit wall,
as you hauled packs to Chimney Pond.

Crafty Black Bear, you composed
that spring at a garage piano, your bulk
squeezed among magazines, lawnmowers
and junk — hovered over paper, pen
and parts while spongy trails to the north
puddled below tree line from snow`s
slow trickle out of its shaded crust.

Back in city rehearsal rooms
you harangued each instrument for us
who came to your house the night before
to splash gin and stuff good food.

Thunderous crack, head tilted back —
is this a storm outside the hall
in Philadelphia or a stack of white
to gray over Katahdin, its tableland
of rubble rock, a flow of ice, the sacred

loaf? Clouds gather in the valleys, stones grind
under foot, tumbling to the sea.

Applause and standing bravos fill the hall:
you stride into the wings, come back to bow
then vanish from the stage, to a hush of sound.

Elegy for a Friend who Climbed Mountains

On our way home I drove
down beside the West Branch of the
Penobscot River below Ripogenus Dam toward
Millinocket. At Abol Bridge rose up the great one,
Katahdin, in unclouded sun, the Great White Whale,
Faulkner's Bear. Brother, I loved you
fifty years. Tight thick muscles,
belly of a walrus or the aging cleric,
no other way to say it, a giant
mind like the mountain, fierce,
cleansed by the hardest wind
on this earth, and maybe any other.
I don't know much, but
that pile of rock's
going to be there
for a long time.

Madison Gulf

We begin fast over a high
suspended bridge, then
smaller fordings that

clean us from the roads
and towns below. Five-thousand footers
lean over us. As we climb their base,

across bouldered streams,
the depths sound our leaps,
tunnels of trees engulf us.

Wind that bends their tops
pulses in the cliff above
like a freight train straining

up a mountain grade.
I'm panting on this pitch —
give me your hand.

As the wall steepens and your hands
fumble in the rock, I hold out
an open palm for you.

Overhead, through the col,
could that be two
trains pounding by

in opposite directions?
We creep up to them and lean into the roar.
I've labored as far as I can go

and still return in daylight.
I know the summit rears open rock
straight up and it's your last chance.

One generation back you turned back
from this peak. This time you choose to go on.
You understand I can't go with you.

I've got sons and daughters
and they've got more to track after you
some day over this ridge of rock, but

not just like you ever again, not just like
this freight-train charge that bends the Arctic grass
over your foot-prints, smaller and smaller

toward the outcropping where
I lose you as you stumble
over mist-glazed rock.

At Bosebuck Mountain Camps

Each morning thunder and rain awaken us,
strings of mist stroke the hills,
and the arms of clouds open out
to what will be a sunny day.
At dusk flocks of swallows
pluck rings on the still surface

of the lake. Stroking without sound
in the canoe, we shock him
poised at a marshy shore.
When he spots our silent slide
he plunges to left, then right
like a downfield runner between

waterline and woods. We share his fear,
alert as the schools of minnows that spread
from his scrambled marks of panic
in the shallows. His leaving swells
the dark, sparked by lightning puffs, then
he's gone into animate night.

Windblown Mountain Pond

The summit's voice
returns edged with granite
when it shouts across the water.
Wild cranberries, tundra flowers
swell the shore and trickle

into the pond. Like a gate
from the underworld, a mouth
upturned thunders words
to the domed sky. Giant's teeth,
shore rocks prickle the haze.

The sodden sky shouts back
an alarm to the cliff face,
laughs outside its blue-grayest
self, its smokiness until
it weeps into the ogre's eyes.

This Weather Is No Womb

Blowing snow tightens cheeks,
says: you move, get inside,
light a fire, don't let it go out;
if you lie down, let the fire go out,
you die. This weather is no womb,
no lush jungle, no springy moss;
it's a slap from the polar ice cap.

Flumes of snow spume and shift
in cloud drift, like waterfall pouring
off the edge of the mountain ridge.
Why does that waver over ice cliff
speed the heart, light the eye?

These white columns make no sense.
We were born in the sucking sea,
these peaks are where we die,
not where we come from but where we go,
the long journey over rock and snow to the pole.

It is night. We have come from the sun
and soon now it will rise and light
that great dark beneath the ice.

Notes

I. THIS BLADE OF LIFE

This section is for Phyllis Towle. It is prefaced with a photo of the author taken by his father, referenced in "The Year We Fell in Love" (p. 17).

II. TO HAVE SEEN THE CHILDREN

This section is prefaced with a photo by Paula Wolcott entitled "Honduran Family, El Rosario, Yoro Province."

P. 34: "The Hitchhiker" is for Beverly Van Orman.

P. 35: "The Drive to Putnamville" is set due north of Montpelier, VT.

III. CONSTANT ENCOUNTERS WITH THE IMPOSSIBLE

The photo introducing this section (of the author's mother and grandniece) is entitled "Pearl Towle and Hannah Parker." It was taken by the author.

P. 53: "A Young Boy Ponders His Death" is in memory of Frank Towle.

P. 55: "Mary Fletcher Hospital, 1958" is in memory of Cynthia Amato. The hospital (now Fletcher Allen Health Care) was and remains a major clinical teaching facility of the University of Vermont, College of Medicine, Burlington, VT.

P. 61: "Requiem for a Marine and His Mate" is in memory of Eunice and George Cunningham.

P. 63: "Buck" is for Dottie and Duncan Aspinwall.

P. 67: "Dusk, a Stream, and a White Owl Cigar" is in memory of Betty Bartlett.

P. 69: "To a Friend Who Loves Trucks" is for Jim Gage.

P. 70: "Elegy for Taylor" is in memory of H. Taylor Caswell, M.D.

P. 72: "A Drowning." The events of this poem occurred on Lake Memphremagog, which spans the border between Vermont and Quebec.

P. 73: "The Willey House Disaster in the Words of Lucy Crawford": from *Lucy Crawford's History of the White Mountains,* Stearns Morse, editor.

P. 77: "The Architecture of Nine-Eleven" comes with a thank-you to Pat Gurney. The professor, Vincent Scully, confirms by post that in the main this description is accurate.

P. 78: "Hooking Rugs and Ice Fishing" is for Donald Sheehan.

P. 80: "Variations on a Riff by Eubie Blake, Dead Age 100, 1984." The quotation is from W. H. Auden's "Massacre of the Innocents."

IV. A JOY GRUMBLING UP

The photo introducing this section was taken by the author and is entitled "Peter Towle at Russell Pond, Baxter State Park (Mt. Katahdin)."

P. 93: "Autumn Dusk Beside the River" is for Paula Wolcott.

P. 94: "Mount Mansfield, Age Eight." Italicized phrases describe Limbo and are from the John Ciardi translation of Dante's *Inferno*, Canto IV.

P. 97: "'Ktaadn': the Premiere" is in memory of Bruce Archibald. Henry David Thoreau used this old Penobscot spelling of "Katahdin" in *The Maine Woods*, describing his journey to the mountain in 1846.

P. 100: "Madison Gulf" is in memory of Berton Towle. The Gulf lies between Mount Adams and Mount Madison in New Hampshire's Presidential Range.

P. 102: "At Bosebuck Mountain Camps" is in memory of Ruth Towne, who "animates the night." The poem is set at the north end of Aziscoos Lake, which transects the Maine-New Hampshire line near the Canadian border.

P. 103: "Windblown Mountain Pond." The poem is set at Harrington Pond, a small, remote body of water high on South Kinsman in the White Mountains, immediately below a particularly challenging section of the Appalachian Trail. To quote the Appalachian Mountain Club guidebook, "The trail…climbs a steep pitch…then struggles up a very steep and rough pitch…which is very exposed to the weather."

About the Author

Parker Towle has published three poetry chapbooks and has edited an anthology of unpublished poems entitled *Exquisite Reaction*. As an Associate Editor of *The Worcester Review*, he has edited special features on Frank O'Hara and Stanley Kunitz. For twenty-five years he was on the board of The Frost Place in Franconia, New Hampshire, and taught at its summer festival.

A member of the Dartmouth-Hitchcock Clinic, he teaches and practices neurology in the north country of New Hampshire and Vermont. In the 1990's he founded a Free Clinic in Littleton, New Hampshire, and volunteered at medical clinics in rural Honduras. He has written and lectured on the interrelationship of medicine and the arts.

With family and friends, Parker Towle has hiked since childhood in the northern New England mountains, and he flails away at a racquetball with poetic abandon. He resides with his wife of fifty-two years in Franconia, New Hampshire.

COLOPHON

This book has been set in Perpetua, designer Eric Gill's most celebrated typeface. The clean, chiseled look of this font recalls its creator's stonecutting work.

To order additional copies of
THIS WEATHER IS NO WOMB
or other Antrim House titles
contact the publisher at

Antrim House
P.O. Box 111
Tariffville, CT 06081
860-217-0023
www.AntrimHouseBooks.com
AntrimHouse@comcast.net

For discussion topics & writing suggestions, as well as additional biography, images and poems for many Antrim House books, visit the Seminar Room of the Antrim House website:
www.AntrimHouseBooks.com/seminar.